AF615232

JUMBO
JACK'S COOKBOOKS
AUDUBON MEDIA CORPORATION
301 BROADWAY • AUDUBON IA 50025
1-800-798-2635

LOST & BURIED TREASURES of the MISSOURI RIVER

by

Netha Bell

QUIXOTE PRESS

Bruce Carlson
31798 K18S
Sioux City, IA
51109

Some of these stories use fictitious names. In those cases, it should be understood that any similarity between those names and actual people, living or dead, is purely coincidental.

* * * * * * * * * * *

QUIXOTE PRESS

Bruce Carlson
31798 K18S
Sioux City, IA
51109

PRINTED IN U.S.A.

DEDICATION

I wish to dedicate this book to the memory of my mother and father, Elizabeth and Pearl Carter, who whetted my interest in the fascinating world of treasure hunting.

ACKNOWLEDGEMENTS

I would like to acknowledge all of the ladies at both libraries . . . Idol Rashid and Cattermole . . . for all the help they have given me in research and the securing of books through the interlibrary system.

Also, I would like to acknowledge Bruce Carlson, my publisher, for his encouragement in my writing endeavors.

TABLE OF CONTENTS

FOREWORD

Netha Bell has pulled together some fascinating accounts of lost treasure in and near our Missouri River. She has found some of the background details that give these accounts some human dimensions. She reminds us that our history is a history of individuals.

Professor Phil Hey
Briar Cliff College
Sioux City, Iowa

PREFACE

The Missouri River is the longest North American river, flowing 2,714 miles to join the Mississippi 17 miles north of St. Louis. Historically, it has been a highway and a boundary. In frontier days, the Missouri marked the line where the West began. The mouth of the Missouri was discovered in 1673 by Marquette and Jolliet. The early fur traders traveled this great river, and, during the late 1700's, began to explore its upper reaches. Lewis and Clark followed the entire course on their way to the Pacific Ocean.

The first river boats were dugout canoes and "bullboats" made of buffalo hide. Next came the keelboats, powered by poles or towed by animals or men walking along its banks. This was very difficult, for the Missouri was a dangerous river. It not only had very powerful currents, but was full of snags, rapids, and sandbars. It is alleged that the Missouri mules got their cussedness from drinking the Missouri River water.

The first steamboat appeared on the Missouri River in 1819. However, with the coming of the railroad in the 1870's, river traffic was reduced. Today, the Missouri is again an important waterway.

The Omaha Indians called the Missouri "Smoky River" because when the river was low, the sandbars were often dry, and when the wind was high, clouds of sand blinded them. These clouds, when seen from afar, looked like smoke.

Some say the word "Missouri" comes from an Illinois dialect of the Algonguian stock and means "wooden canoe".

Whatever its origin, the word is colorful sounding and suggests the rush, the wildness, and mystery of the river!!

CHAPTER ONE

THE KNIFE RIVER CACHE

legion of propectors descended on Montana when gold was discovered. This discovery was one of the prinicpal causes of Indian unrest along the upper Missouri River. That, coupled with engineers crisscrossing the Sioux territory seeking potential wagon routes, caused trouble. Steamboats were bringing more white men into the Indian's territory.

The Sioux were a powerful and warlike people, proud, haughty, and defiant. The warriors averaged about six-feet in height, with strong, muscular frames. They were also good horsemen. The white man was looked upon as a threat to the red man's buffalo, elk, deer and antelope which abounded in their country.

In the heyday of Montana mining, it became customary for prospectors to return home each fall by means of mackinaw boats. These were quickly and cheaply built, and only suitable for a single trip.

In the late fall of 1864, one such boat carried sixteen miners returning from the gold fields of Montana. Three of the miners . . . Ezra Pike, Thomas Brady, and Norbert Heygood, were going to Sioux City, Iowa. They had gone upriver on the "Emilie" that spring. Now, after a successful six months, they were going home.

Ezra Pike was a big, raw-boned man, with a weather-beaten face. This was mostly due to a life spent in the out-of-doors. He'd been . . . at various time . . . a farmer, trapper, lumberjack, fisherman and hunter, before trying his luck at prospecting.

Thomas Brady was the least likely looking prospector of the trio. He was short, too fat around the middle, and bald. He sweated profusely upon exertion . . . no matter what the season.

Norbert Heygood was a wiry, rather non-descript man of medium height and build. He lent little to any conversation . . . whether out of shyness or an aversion to talking.

Their journey down the Missouri was long and

tedious. They'd pull their boat ashore at night and make camp. Ezra, being the most experienced hunter of the group, usually supplied game for their supper. Once in a while they would camp more than one night in an area. And always . . . whether on the river or in the camp . . . they had to be on the lookout for Indians.

The miners had pulled their boat ashore at a point where the Knife River enters the Missouri near the present town of Stanton, North Dakota.

It was a likely looking spot. Game was seen before they could even disembark. While the others were unloading the boat, as they intended to camp for a few days, Ezra Pike grabbed his gun and took off for the woods. He was back shortly with several quail and a pheasant.

"I tell ya, I never seen so much game in mah life!!" Ezra remarked. "Gonna go back out soon as supper's over and git some more. 'Nuff ta last fer a couple of days, at least."

Although not fancy, the miners had a rib-stickin' meal of stew, roast quail and pheasant, and pan-fried cornbread. Conversation was lively, mostly about what they were going to do once they got home.

"Whatcha donna do with all yer gold, Thomas?" Ezra asked.

"First, I'm gonna git that sweet little wife of mine the purtiest dress I can buy. And all the trimmins!! Shoes, bonnet, jewelry and a new purse. Then I'm gonna git me a new horse and buggy . . . all fancy-like!!"

The other men smiled, thinking about what they had in mind for their share of the $200,000 they had accumluated.

"Hey, Norbert, what 'er ya gonna do with yers?" Ezra asked.

"Do with my what?" Norbert inquired.

"Damn!! Is yer head in the clouds again? What we bin talkin' about, man? Yer gold, that's what!!" Ezra yelled.

"Oh, well, I hadn't given it much thought," Norbert answered.

Ezra just rolled his eyes upward and shook his head. He wasn't sure that Norbert had both oars in the water!!

"Well, men, I'm goin' out huntin' 'gin. Might as well git some more of that there game fer it gits too dark ta see. Y'all can clean up and ah think ya better bury that gold, so's we don't have ta worry 'bout it while we're here."

With this, Ezra Pike stood up and stretched. He rubbed his belly, saying, "Mighty good eatin'. Well, I'd better git goin'."

After Ezra had left, some of the miners got busy cleaning up the remains of the meal. Others took their gold into the woods, as Ezra had advised. They went a ways and buried it. As each man was occupied with a task, a band of Indians rode into the encampment. The sound of Ezra's hunting had alerted them that the white man had invaded their country again. They were hell-bent on wreaking vengeance!!

With a self-satisfied smile on his face from having some good luck in hunting, Ezra broke through the clearing to the encampment. His smile quickly changed to one of horror when he saw the sight before him!! The Indians had done their job well!!! Fifteen miners . . . friends . . . lay slaughtered around the camp. The only sign of life was the bonfire giving off wisps of smoke.

"My God!! Oh, my God!!" Ezra cried, as he let the deer slide off his shoulders and sank to his knees.

Finally managing to stand up, he went on into the camp.

A swift glance of where the gold has been told Ezra that the other miners had taken his advice and buried it. But where?? Probably in the woods, someplace. At this point, the prospector decided that he was not going to stick around and look for the gold. Not knowing just how close the Indians were, he quickly loaded the boat with a few provisions. With much struggling, he was able to get the boat afloat and jumped in. He wasn't sure how he'd manage the boat by himself, but he felt safer than on foot.

Somewhere, on the south bank of the Missouri at its confluence with the Knife River, and just north of the town of Stanton, North Dakota, lies

$200,000 in gold, just waiting to be found!!

CHAPTER TWO

THE COUNCIL BLUFFS TRAIN ROBBERY

t was a cold, blustery, latė fall day in Omaha. Two young men from Council Bluffs, Iowa, Merle Phillips and Fred Poffenbarger, Jr., were whiling away time at the "Eight-Ball Poolroom". Both were railroad men and this was their day off. So, they had

decided to come over and shoot a few games. They had each won a game and were just sitting around, having a drink and relaxing.

"Ya know, Fred, I've bin thinkin'," said Merle to his companion. "I think there's a way to come up with more money than we just won on those pool games."

"Oh, yeah? How's that?" Fred inquired.

Merle looked around to see if anyone was close enough to overhear their conversation. Satisfied that there wasn't, he continued.

"Well . . . when I'm sortin' that mail, I git to thinkin' . . . there's an awful lot of money and stuff in those mail pouches!!" Merle said.

"Yeah . . . I s'pose. But what's that got to do with us?" Fred asked.

"If we could just git our hands on those pouches, I bet we'd have enough money to go to Florida and git out of this cold weather," Merle advised.

"Aw, yer out of yer mind!!" Fred remarked.

"No, I ain't!" Merle countered. "I think it could be done."

They sat there, discussing ideas on how they might pull this thing off. Putting their heads together, they came up with a plan. Merle'd ride "shotgun" as lookout on the engine tender. When the train stopped for a crossing, a window to the treasure car could be smashed and the pouches thrown out.

" 'Course, we'd have to git a couple of guys with cars drivin' along-side the train. They'd git the pouches and take off," Merle said.

So, it was decided that they'd ask Keith Collins, a fireman on the train, to throw in with them. He had a car and maybe he knew someone else with one that would be willing to help.

The first chance he had, Merle talked to Keith, who seemed to like the idea. And yes, he knew this guy named Roberts that just might be interested in going along. Now, all they had to do was figure out when this was going to come off!!

On Saturday, November 11, 1920, the plan was put into action. It was pulled off without a hitch, except one mail pouch was dropped. But the drivers escaped with the rest.

The real clincher was when Merle realized that those dirty dogs weren't going to divvy up the loot with him. Red-faced from anger and mumbling to himself, he made his decision to rat on those punks!!

The officials had already come to the conclusion that this had to be an "inside job", because it had been worked out too well. They felt that most bandits would not have known which car contained the loot. Various branches of law enforcement took up the manhunt for the others involved.

Fred Poffenbarger, Jr. and the man named Roberts were arrested. Now the authorities focused their attention on Keith Collins. His trail led them to Westville, Oklahoma, to the home of his uncle.

Collins was dirty and unkempt at the time of his arrest. It was alleged that Collins had escaped with over $3,000,000 in bonds. This was supposed to include 100 shares of General Motors and 50 shares of Kennecott Copper stocks.

"I didn't think we could sell 'em, so I put all of 'em in a suitcase. Then I put in some lead weights. After I drove to the Douglas St. Bridge, I got out and walked about half-way across the bridge. Then I stopped and thought . . . Ya know, you're crazy, throwin' away all that money!! I almost backed out but decided if we couldn't sell 'em, what the hell good were they to us? So, I threw that suitcase in the middle of the Missouri River!!"

The money taken in the robbery was recovered, but there are no records showing that the suitcase has ever been found!!

CHAPTER THREE

THE CENTRALIA CACHES

ill Anderson and his band of bushwhackers were notorious around the time of the Civil War. Anderson, born in Randolph County, Missouri, moved with his parents and two sisters to Johnson County, Kansas, where it is said he lived quietly as a farmer in 1862. According to Hampton Watts, a member of his band, the tragic deaths of Anderson's sisters in Kansas City, after their arrests and imprisonment as Confederate sympathizers, and the murder of his father, caused him to "take up arms against his government." The dramatic forays, and at times, barbarous cruelties of Bill Anderson and his men, became legendary.

Centralia, Missouri, is located in Boone County and lies just north of the Missouri River. It was so named for its central position on the railroad between St. Louis, Missouri, and Ottumwa, Iowa.

During the Civil War, it was The location of the Centralia Massacre.

On the fateful morning of September 27, 1864, a band of 80 Confederate guerillas, led by the infamous Bill Anderson, entered the town of Centralia. After plundering the two stores, they started in on the homes for more supplies and food.

A stagecoach, with the misfortune of having just arrived from Columbia, Missouri, was held up, and the passengers robbed. Aboard was James S. Rollins, a U.S. congressman, and James H. Waugh, the sheriff of Boone County, both strong Union sympathizers. But, surprisingly, none of the guerillas or the leader were recognized.

While the robbery was in progress, the guerillas' attention was diverted by the approach of a North Missouri train from St. Louis. They abandoned the stagecoach and hurriedly placed ties across the railroad tracks to stop the engine. They then opened fire, wounding the fireman.

Amongst the passengers on board were a couple of dozen unarmed Federal soldiers who were either on furlough or had been recently discharged. The bandits robbed the passengers and then took $3,000 from the baggage car safe. Next, they rifled the passengers' baggage, taking at least $10,000 from one piece of luggage.

After the group evacuated the train, along with the passengers, they set fire to it. They then forced the engineer to open the throttle. The blazing train traveled two or three miles west before it was entirely burned.

Bill Anderson then ordered the Federal soldiers shot. The depot was burned and the guerilla group returned to their nearby camp with their

spoils. Included in their loot from the stores was a large supply of liquor, which they immediately delved into to celebrate their "victory".

That same afternoon, Major A.V.E. Johnson led a force of 175 Union soldiers into Centralia. He was under the impression that the size of the guerilla band was highly overestimated and decided to pursue them. He gathered 140 men in the open prairies, leaving 35 men to guard the town of Centralia.

Meanwhile, the guerillas sent out a small scouting party under the leadership of Dave Poole. Their purpose was to lure the Union soldiers into the guerillas' encampment. Major

Johnson and his men took the bait, fell into the trap and were attacked. The battle lasted a short time but was furiously fought. The Union soldiers were mostly raw recruits, poorly trained and equipped. The guerillas were trained marksmen, who had fresh horses and were all armed.

Major Johnson was killed and not more than a dozen of his men managed to escape.

The area of this bloody battle has produced many relics and it is belived that many caches of Bill Anderson's loot and valuables await recovery in this region.

CHAPTER FOUR

BEHIND THOSE SWINGIN' DOORS

ertram Clark and Hiram Ingles were saloonkeepers in Leavenworth, Kansas, during the 1850's. They had grown up together in Ohio and neither had much schooling, nor had either one married. The pair were big, robust men. They had worked hard, lived frugally and decided to "go west, young men". Pooling their savings, the friends bought a saloon. They did a "fair-to-middlin'" business from locals and travelers who wanted to quench their thirsts.

Then along came the discovery of gold at Sutter's Mill in January of 1848 by James Marshall. When rumors of the discovery reached eastern newspapers, those easterners caught the gold fever. They struck off for the west by the thousands, singing to the tune of "Oh, Susanna":

"I shall soon be in San Francisco and then I'll look around, and when I see the gold lumps there I'll pick them off the ground!!"

Some 80,000 gold hunters poured into California. A lot of those hunters passed through the swinging door of Clark and Ingles' saloon on their way to the "Land of Gold", increasing business considerably.

But a few years later, when the prospectors started returning home after having struck it rich, Clark and Ingles got greedy. Seeing all that gold dust and nuggets made them come to a decision. They were going gold-hunting . . . right in their own saloon!! With the foregone conclusion that two heads were better than one, they put theirs together and came up with a plan.

Whenever a "loner" came into the saloon and flashed some of his takings around, Bertram would keep feeding him drinks. If it was early in the evening, he made sure the prospector wasn't too drunk until nearer closing time. Then they'd close up the saloon and invite the man to "bunk over at our place and sleep it off until mornin'."

The man usually accepted the invitation, unaware that it spelled out his death warrant. Come morning, he'd be gone and Clark and Ingles would be that much richer.

One evening, a man by the name of Martin O'Brien came into the saloon. He wasn't the usual unkempt prospector. He even appeared to have seen a barber recently. Sitting by himself, Martin did not engage in the usual boasting of "striking it rich" like so many of Clark and Ingles' customers. He answered briefly when spoken to, but lent little to any conversation. But he did pay for his drinks in gold coins.

His drinks . . . that was something which bothered the saloonkeepers! Martin wasn't drinking any of their "red-eyed" whiskey. No, sir, he was sipping on sassparilla!! Can ya imagine, the very thought . . . sassparilla!! Thet's only fer wimmin and li'l kids!! No real man wud be caught daid drinkin' that sissy-stuff!! Further, it sure done posed a problem! Jest how in the hell was they gonna git him drunk? Clark and Ingles put their heads together again.

The hour was late and business had slacked off considerably. The two men had had a very profitable day, but now it was time to attend to the business of Martin. He was just sitting there, sipping on the last of his sassparilla. Clark offered him a fresh one . . . on the house. Martin accepted. The only other customer had just left when Martin asked if there was a hotel close.

"Nope," Clark answered. "But there's a roomin' house jest down the street aways. But iffen ya want, we've gotta spare bed ya kin bunk down in."

"Naah, I don't wanna put ya out," Martin remarked.

"No trouble atall," Ingles put in. "Glad to have ya."

The barkeeps tidied up a bit, then locked up. The three started off towards their house.

"Didn't drink yur last sassparilla," Clark observed.

"Nope. I decided I'd had enuff," Martin informed him.

This presented the two another problem, as Martin's drink had been poisoned!! Now, how were they going to get rid of this guy? Guess they'd just have to see how it went after they got to the house.

"Wud ya lika drink?" Clark asked of Martin.

"Never touch the stuff," the prospector replied.

"How 'bout a cuppa coffee or tea?"

"No, thanks. Don't drink them, either."

Well, they thought, poison's out completely, then. Now what??

"If ya don't mind . . . my bones are pritty weary. I'd jest like to go ta bed," Martin informed the pair. "Gotta git on my way in the mornin'."

Clark exchanged a questioning look with Ingles. He couldn't think of any way short of violence to do in their "guest".

"Sure. We understand. Let me show ya whur ya kin sleep," said Clark, moving towards the bedroom. "Jest put yer stuff in here. Hope ya git a good night's rest."

After Martin had gone into the room and closed the door, Clark motioned for Ingles to follow him into the kitchen.

"Whut we gonna do?" Clark asked in a whisper.

"We could shoot him, but that'd bring in the law, more'n likely."

"No, no! We dunt wanna do thet! Sumbody'd be in her quicker than lightnin'!! Gotta figger out sumthin' else.

"How's 'bout smotherin' him with a pillar?" Ingles asked.

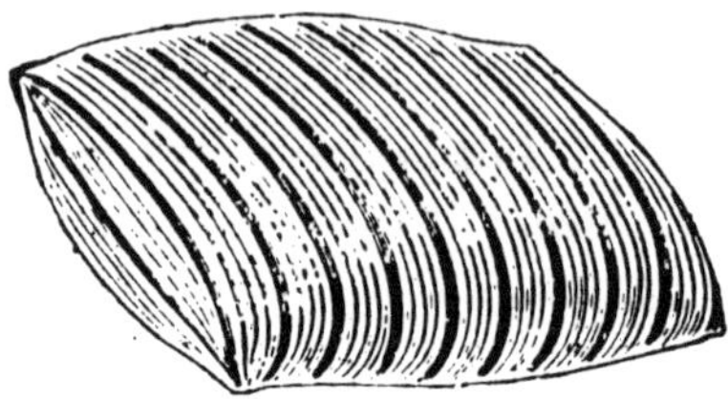

"Hey, now, Hiram old buddy, maybe ya done thought of sumthin' for onced in yer life," Clark remarked excitedly. "Who's gonna do it . . . you or me?"

"Since I done thunk it up, you shud be ther one to do it."

So it was agreed that Clark would wait until he was sure that Martin had been asleep for a little while before putting the plan into action. Since their "guest" wasn't too big, they didn't think he'd give them much trouble. But this was one time that the sayings "Don't judge a book by its cover" and "Big things come in small packages" might have applied.

Meanwhile, Martin had gone to bed with all his clothes on as he had a feeling something might happen. He had put his gun under the pillow just in case. The prospector had checked the door first thing. Naturally, it wouldn't lock. Not much he could do about that except stay alert.

Perhaps an hour or so later, Martin thought he heard footsteps in the hall. He started snoring as if asleep and squinted his eyes towards the doorway. He heard the door creak as it was slowly opened. He reached under the pillow for the gun. Footsteps moved stealthfully toward the bed. He positioned his hand holding the gun. The

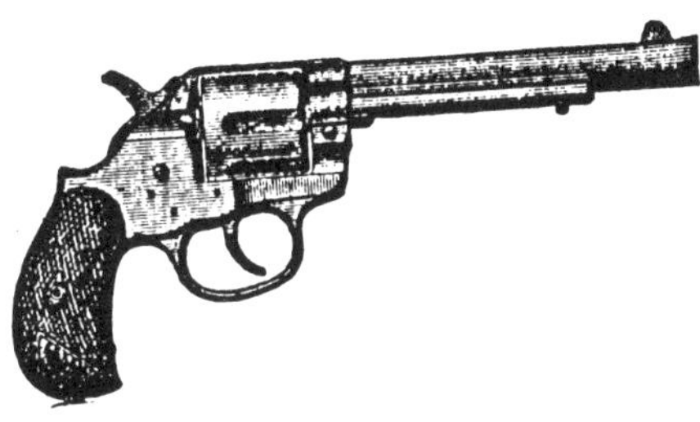

figure had moved between him and the faint light of the window. Just as Clark was getting ready to cover Martin's face with the pillow, the prospector rolled to the other side of the bed and leaped out, aiming his gun.

"Stay right where ya are or I'll pull this trigger!!"

Martin rushed around the foot of the bed so fast that the lumbering Clark barely had time to move. Caught totally by surprise, he'd not thought of his next course of action. Martin hit him above his left ear with the butt of the gun, causing Clark to fall to the floor unconscious.

Martin O'Brien hurried down the hall . . . then stopped to see if he could either hear or see Ingles. He heard loud snoring from behind a closed door and assumed that he wouldn't be stopped. Opening the front door, he took off at a dead-run to the sheriff's office.

Ingles was still asleep . . . and, as a matter of fact, so was Clark . . . when the authorities arrived. The two saloonkeepers gave little resistance.

Martin O'Brien was a Federal Investigator trying to find out what had become of the many prospectors that had disappeared. The trail led back to the Clark and Ingles saloon.

The two men were jailed, but vigilantes, upon hearing of the crimes committed by the pair, stormed the jail when the sheriff was gone. Before he returned, the saloonkeepers had been strung up by the outraged group. Only afterwards was it learned that neither of the two had told where their spoils were buried. Although much searching was done, nothing has ever been found!!

CHAPTER FIVE

THE KANSAS CITY WOODEN BOX TREASURE

ack in 1864 Father Bernard Donnelly was the priest of the Church of the Immaculate Conception in Kansas City, Missouri. It was a period of unrest. As the Confederate army approached their city, half the populace frantically withdrew their money from the banks.

"We've worked too long and hard for someone to take it from us!!" seemed to be the consensus of opinion.

Many of the congregation of the church turned to the one person they could trust . . . Father Donnelly. Discussions were held and a meeting was called. Herman Dundee was the spokesman for the group.

"Father Donnelly . . . as you know, the Confederate troops are on their way here. Most of us fear that we will be robbed of our hard-earned money and valuables. Do you have any idea where we can safely hide them?"

There was a flurry of conversation in agreement with what Herman had just said.

"Perhaps everything would be safe here in the church. Surely the troops wouldn't descecrate God's house . . . would they?" asked the priest.

"We've thought of that, Father. But we're afraid they would!! Is there anyplace else you can think of where we can store our things?" Herman asked.

"Hmmm. Yes, I think I have an idea," Father Donnelly remarked.

That night, the hoard of accumulated valuables was put into a large wooden box. With the help

of the grave digger, Pete O'Dell, Father Donnelly used a wheelbarrow to take the box to the cemetery two blocks west of the church, where they proceeded to bury it.

The grave digger had a habit of talking too much after a few drinks. After helping the good Father with his chore, the man felt in need of a little libation. Going to his favorite saloon, "Digger O'Dell" got involved in a lively conversation with a few well-known rowdies. A member of the congregation overheard "Digger" telling the rowdies about hiding the valuables. The man hurried to the church and told Father Donnelly.

The priest . . . even though worn out from the previous burial . . . enlisted the help of a few trusted parishoners. They dug up the wooden box and carted it back to the churchyard. Marking off measurements to the north of the church, they reburied the treasure in a plowed field.

It had rained for several days, but when things had quieted down, Father Donnelly returned to the site to recover the hoard which belonged to his flock. But try as he might, he could not locate the place where the box had been buried. Frantically searching . . . clear up to the day he died . . . all his efforts proved fruitless. There is no record of this wooden box ever having been found!!

CHAPTER SIX

TREASURE HUNTER'S DELIGHT

s any treasure hunter knows, to uncover even one cache in a certain area is considered good odds. But how about an area that could contain anywhere from one to one hundred caches! The chance is very good, and the caches range in value from $100 to $1,000. Although they would mostly be in coins, several would be in gold dust.

Sarpy County, Nebraska, is in the extreme eastern part of the state. A field of five to ten acres lies about three miles west of Plattsmouth. This was used as a camping ground for over twenty years by gold seekers either on their way to or from the western gold fields.

When gold was discovered on Cherry Creek, Colorado, in 1850, a steady stream of hopeful prospectors passed through Plattsmouth for several

years. This was one of the last places the men could stop for supplies. Thousands of them outfitted here before going west. Store owners of

Plattsmouth fired these greenhorn prospectors' desire for gold by telling them that within a month or two they'd be back with a fortune!!

These gullible easterners would listen with their mouths agape. They paid in coin for their supplies to mine the supposedly large amounts of gold in Colorado. But their big dreams were dashed when the hard work to grub out $3.00

worth of gold a day proved to be just too much. True, a few of them were lucky, but most of them barely saved enough to make it back home.

By 1859, several thousand disillusioned miners had passed through Plattsmouth on their way back east. One group of over 1,000 miners camped at the usual place. Those that had gold or coins, buried their caches near the campsites. A good many of the ex-miners were angry with the merchants of Plattsmouth, as they felt they had been tricked into buying supplies. So, that evening, they made plans to rob and burn the town.

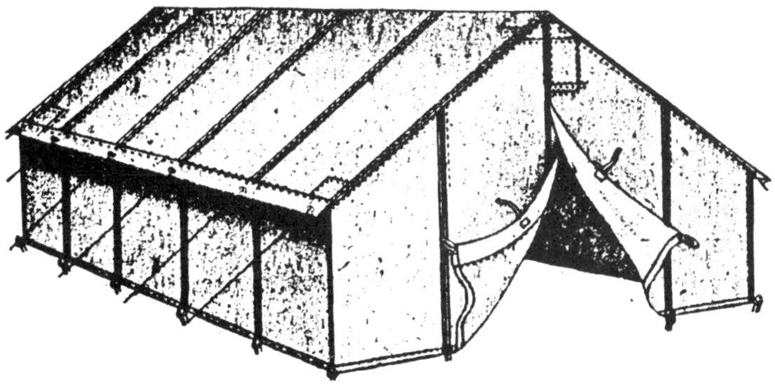

This group of men gathered the next morning, intending to sack Plattsmouth. Before they left the campground, however, those miners that had not buried their valuables previously, did so then.

But apparently someone had tipped off the people of the town. When the miners reached the edge of Plattsmouth, they met armed citizens just waiting for them.

Before the ex-prospectors realized what was going on, they were being driven to the Missouri River. There they were told to "Swim to Iowa and don't come back!!" Having little choice, the miners crossed the river however they could.

After being sure that all miners had crossed the river, a bunch of Plattsmouth's citizens went to the campground. There, they took in a scene of abandonment. Wagons, mules, horses, mining

tools and camping equipment were just where the miners had left them. The citizens took some of the things, but the rest of the litter could be seen for years.

Some of the townspeople knew the miners had cached their gold and valuables, but did not know where. A few searches were made, but there is no record of these caches being found. It is known that few miners ever returned.

Today, someone using a metal detector could have a good chance of finding one or more of these cahces. Happy hunting!!

CHAPTER SEVEN

THE FRANCIS X. AUBREY

arkville, Missouri, is a small college town in the Kansas City metropolitan area. In the early 1840's, it was one of the most important towns on the north bank of the Missouri River. It surpassed even Kansas City.

On August 10, 1865 . . . having left St. Louis nine days previously . . . the riverboat "Francis X. Aubrey" was near Parkville. Suddenly, without warning, the "Aubrey" hit a snag that ripped her hull from stem to stern!! The vessel drifted

a short distance, finally running into the river bank across from the old Summer's farm. Luckily, all 130 passengers safely left the boat before it started to sink into the waters of the Missouri River. But crewmen were unable to unload any of its cargo, which consisted of pottery, wagons, clothing and some 500 barrels of whiskey. There was also an undetermined amount of gold bullion and coins . . . although one source shows it at $500,000!!

Just before the turn of the century, Gale Henson . . . the mayor of Holt, Missouri . . . called a meeting of some of his friends.

"Folks . . . I believe most of you know each other . . . I called this meeting for one purpose. Most of you also know that I have a great interest in some of the boats that have had the misfortune of sinking in the Missouri River. Well, now . . . I think I've stumbled onto something that may be very worthwhile . . . and right in our area, too!"

The men exchanged questioning glances . . . at each other and at Gale Henson. There was a flurry of conversation. Then the mayor held up his hands for silence . . . and then continued.

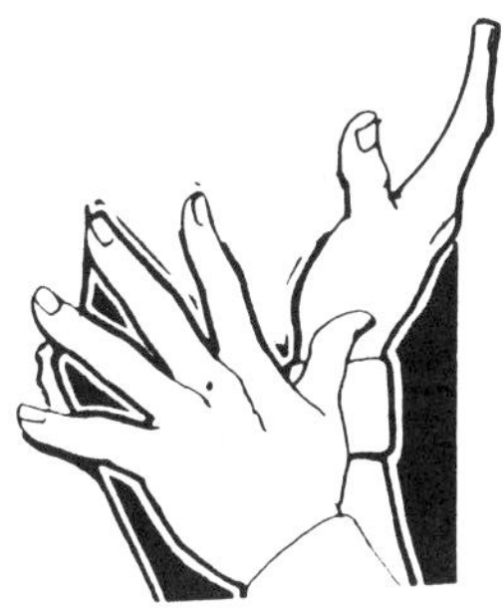

"I know a lot of you think I'm a dreamer. And maybe I am. Or was. But this just might be a dream come true!! Have any of you heard of the steamboat "Francis X. Aubrey"? No? Well, it was a steamer that went down near Parkville. Besides its other cargo, seems that there was about 500 barrels of whiskey aboard. Sure could throw a hell of a party with that, hmm? Oh, yes, and there was also about $500,000 worth of gold coins and bullion aboard. NOW, does THAT interest anyone here??"

There were a lot of affirmative answers . . . both for the whiskey and the gold.

"Sounds like an interesting story, Gale, but just how are we involved?" asked Robert Smith.

"Yeah, Gale. I'd like to know, too," said Dan Peterson.

Several others agreed with the two men.

"Well, folks, that's the whole idea of this meeting. I think we stand a good chance of salvaging this boat and its cargo. Of course, the project will take money. I thought I'd let my friends get in on the opportunity of making great returns on a small investment."

"How do we go about finding this sunken boat?" Smith asked.

"I've researched the area where it sank and it may not be as difficult as it sounds," Henson replied.

"It must be down a long ways by now, isn't it?" Peterson inquired.

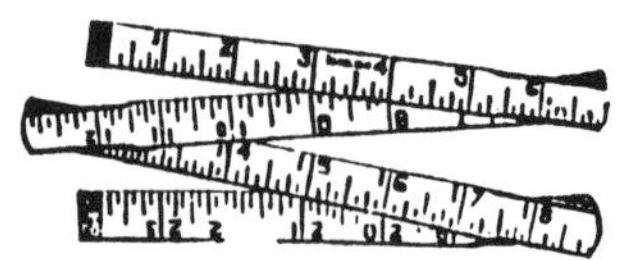

"Maybe . . . maybe not. We'll just have to wait and see."

"We can't just go and start diggin'. What else do you have in mind?" one of the other men asked.

"I think we can probe the river mud with long iron rods and locate it," Henson answered.

There was more discussion regarding who wanted in and who didn't; how much money had to be invested; forming a syndicate; when they were going to start searching, etc. Then the meeting adjourned for the evening.

For weeks the group probed the river mud with rods but found nothing. All the while, Farmer Summers watched their futile efforts.

"Tain't where the boat's at," Summers told them. "Iffen ya cut me in fer a share, I'll show ya where 'tis."

The group mostly ignored him the best they could. Finally, after a few more non-productive tries, they decided to accept the farmer's offer. He led them to a place approximately a mile from the banks of the Missouri River. The searchers started probing this region with the rods and hit some hard objects.

"Hey, I think we hit pay-dirt," one of the men yelled.

They all quit probing and started digging. After much hard work and perspiration, they found what they were looking for. There, under 24-feet of mud, the upper part of a vessel appeared. The hull was buried even deeper.

When word got around that the "Aubrey" had been found, some hopeful, but foolish, investors, thinking that the whiskey might still be good, offered $25,000. But the members of the syndicate turned them down . . . holding out for $50,000!!

Meanwhile, the digging operations continued. At a depth of 30-feet, they began to have problems.

"Damn!!" one of the men yelled. "Water's seepin in!!"

But, at least they had begun to bring up objects . . . such as they were!! Rotted and musty leather boots, bits and pieces of furniture . . . and even the running gear of a wagon. But no whiskey and no money was found!!

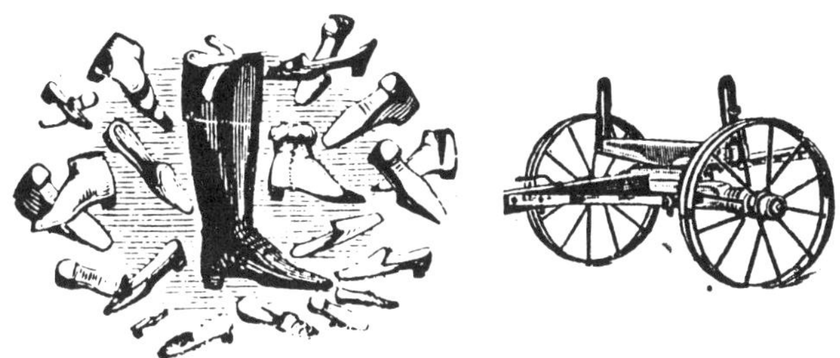

Then the fall rains came and they had to abandon the project temporarily. And wouldn't you know it . . . that winter the "Big Muddy" flooded!! It completely covered the digging site. The next spring, the syndicate could find no trace and could not raise enough money to pursue their endeavor. Disgusted, they called off the whole deal!!

There are no records that indicate any further attempts have been made to recover the treasure since 1897!!

CHAPTER EIGHT

THE RIVERSIDE PARK TREASURES

ierre, the state capital of South Dakota, is located on the eastern bank of the Missouri River in the approximate center of the state. For many years the present city was a ferry landing for the bustling town of Fort Pierre across the river.

In the late 1870's, a party of miners were returning from the Black Hills gold fields. They had accumulated approximately $500,000 in gold dust and nuggets. Fearful of Indians whom they believed were following them, the miners put ashore at Pierre during the night and buried their treasure.

They continued their journey down the Missouri River, intending to return later to recover their cache of gold. Apparently their fears were well founded, as the boatload of miners were attacked by Indians a short ways downstream.

Sometime in the early 1920's, a stranger came to Pierre. He entered into a contract with the city on a fifty-fifty basis to recover the gold. However, there is no record of his having discovered the cache, even though the water was shallow.

Most sources agree that the location is about 100 feet from the banks of the Missouri River and opposite the mouth of the Little River or Bad River. The present-day Riverside City Park is at this location. The cache was supposed to have been buried near a large cottonwood tree.

About 10 years earlier, an unidentified vessel carrying gold bullion was wrecked at the present-day Pierre, before a permanent settlement had been established. Because of Indian unrest, the vessel was never salvaged. The cargo of gold from the Montana mines was valued at $260,000. Reports at the time said the site of the sinking was near three towering cottonwood trees growing close together.

Riverside Park in Pierre is located at Missouri Avenue and Crow Street. There once stood three cottonwood trees in the park which were known as "The Three Sisters".

In 1922, a company was organized to salvage the vessel and its contents. A shaft was sunk in the solid ground near the trees where the river had flowed before changing it course. There is no record of either the boat or gold being found.

The site may be covered by mud and silt in the riverbed or on dry land in the park.

CHAPTER NINE

"MUSTACHE MARIE" PHILLIPS

ayneville is now a ghost town located on the Missouri River just across from Fort Osage. It was a wild, roaring army town that thrived by catering mostly to the soldiers from the fort. By ferryboat in summer and over the ice by bobsled in winter went the soldier, trader, bullwhacker, Indian and cowboy. They all wanted to "taste the night life", which was so abundantly offered in the gaming houses with their expansive bars and friendly hostesses. In Territorial days, there were eight saloons operating. It also had a race track, where many a financial transaction was conducted.

Like other western towns, Payneville attracted a wide variety of inhabitants. This included slim-fingered gamblers, hired killers, and the ever-present madam and her "working girls". These were the types of individuals that did not use the banking facilities. Instead, they were more inclined to use the "post-hole" banks or bury their caches.

One of the most colorful of Payneville's citizens was "Mustache Marie" Phillips, a tall, large and angular young schoolteacher. Although masculine in appearance, she wore women's clothing, except her boots, for which she reportedly paid $20 a pair.

Marie got her nickname from the thin line of facial hair she sported above her upper lip. She did not acquire this unladylike name until she had changed her profession.

Marie had had an unusually tiring day trying to pound reading and writing into the heads of the local children who wanted to be anywhere but in school. At suppertime she was complaining about her thankless job and how discouraging it was. She roomed at a boarding house, as did Jake Larson, a barkeep. He agreed with her that it was a hard job, and that was why it was difficult to keep schoolteachers in Payneville.

"If you're interested in a change of occupations, I have a friend you might like to meet," remarked Jake.

"Sure. Anything would have to be an improvement to teaching. These children just do not seem interested in learning even the fundamentals of reading, writing, and arithmetic. Just what kind of occupation are we discussing?" Marie asked.

"We'll talk about it later, okay, Marie?"

After dessert and coffee, Marie helped clear the table. Then turning to Jake she stated, "You've gotten my curiousity aroused, Jake. I hate to press the issue, but may we talk now? If not, I have a lot of things to do to get ready for class tomorrow."

"Yeah, I guess it's as good a time as any. I've gotta go to work now, anyway, so why don't you just come with me?"

"I'm not really interested in being a barkeep, Jake, if that's what you have in mind," Marie informed him.

"Oh, no, no, I know that, Marie. Trust me," Jake remarked.

The pair walked over to the "Ruby Lady" saloon where Jake worked.

"Marie, I'd like for you to meet Miss Dolly. She's the friend I was talking about. Miss Dolly, this is our latest disillusioned schoolmarm. She may be thinkin' about changin' occupations. Well, girls, I've gotta git to work, so I'll just leave you two to talk."

Miss Dolly was a rather buxom, but attractive woman who wore her red hair in an upsweep. Her lowcut gown showed an ample expanse of mountains and valleys.

"What kind of business do you have, Miss Dolly?" Marie inquired, although she was pretty sure she already knew.

"Well, Marie, let's just say that I run a thriving little business upstairs. This is a more lucrative business than teachin' school."

"You run a brothel, in other words, right?"

"You might say that. I prefer to call it my house of entertainment," Miss Dolly replied.

"But just how would I fit in? I'm certainly no raving beauty, and to be truthful, quite inexperienced," Marie commented. "I'm not even sure that I would know what to do."

"I would give you some basic instructions, my dear. But after a while, I'm sure you would catch on fine."

"Let me think about it, Miss Dolly. I'm not happy with teaching, but . . . well, just let me think it over, okay?"

"Sure, honey, take all the time you need."

Marie left the saloon, positive that everyone in the place knew what she and Miss Dolly had been discussing. She felt her cheeks blazing with embarrassment.

Marie tried to grade the papers, but her conversation with the madam kept creeping into her mind. How could she even consider doing what Miss Dolly had suggested?? And how dare that Jake Larson even implying that she might be interested!! She slept very little that night.

The next day at school was especially tiring. None of the children had done their homework, and they were high-spirited. All in all, Marie's mind kept returning to the possibility of changing her profession. By the end of the day, she had made up her mind.

As soon as she could get the children out of her way, she locked the schoolhouse door for the final time. She then went to see Mr. Spruce who had hired her. Marie gave him the keys and told him that she quit. Mr. Spruce didn't seem too surprised. She then walked to the "Ruby Lady" saloon.

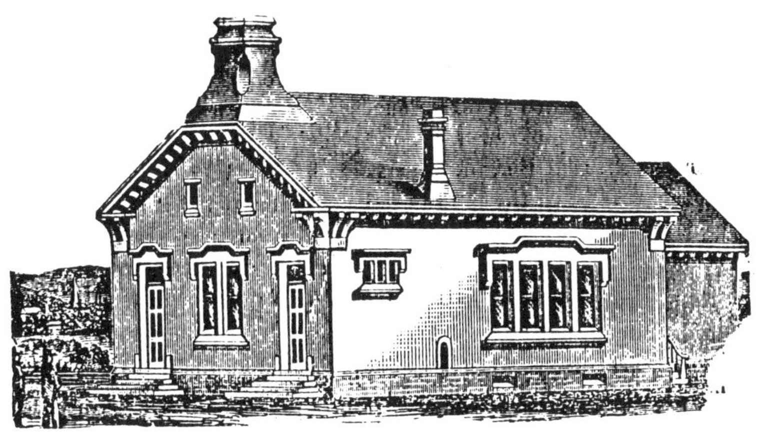

Miss Dolly saw Marie as soon as she came through the door. Giving her a smile, she gestured for Marie to follow her upstairs. They went into the madam's room.

"I quit my job," Marie told Dolly. "I hope to God I didn't do something foolish!!"

"Now, honey, I know it's something you gave a lot of thought. You didn't sleep much last night, did you?"

"Does it show that much?"

"Let's just say that right now, you look like somethin' the cats drug in. But we'll fix that up. Tonight you just get yourself some rest and tomorrow we'll talk, okay?"

Marie went home but slept very fitfully. She was almost glad that her parents had passed away, as she would not have wanted them to see her come down to this after their great expectations.

Marie's life was not an easy one. Because of her new occupation, the women of Payneville ostracized her, but the men found her well-educated, an astute business woman, a good poker player, and an excellent cook.

Before too long, "Mustache Marie" . . . as she was now known . . . became the proprietor of one of Payneville's most scarlet institutions. She collected quite a library and became very adept with a needle.

She met Bart Phillips, a rancher, whom she married. Her interest in her own business declined, so she managed her husband's ranch.

There was another side of life in Payneville. It was an enterprising business town. Besides, it was the center of a growing ranching country. It had a Literary Society and a Dramatic Club. The Sunday School had been organized by Mr. and Mrs. Spruce, who had hired Maude as a teacher. One day, Mr. and Mrs. Spruce, together with four other members of their family, were killed by five drunken Indians. The Indians were subsequently lynched for their crimes.

Marie lived near Payneville until her death.

After the abandonment of Fort Osage, Payneville began to decline. Today, nothing is left of it but a few old cellars and a couple of stands of trees. It is claimed that there are a number of worthwhile caches and "post-hole" banks in the area that have still not been discovered.

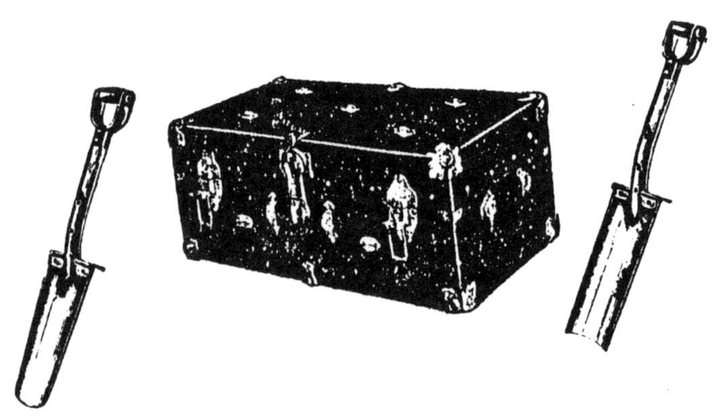

CHAPTER TEN

THE "BERTRAND"

n April 1, 1865, under veteran riverman, Capt. James Yore, the "Bertrand" was making her maiden voyage from St. Louis, up the Missouri River. She was on her way to Fort Benton in the Montana Territory.

On this April Fool's Day, she was just north of the present-day Omaha-Council Bluffs area and was about four miles downstream from DeSoto, Nebraska Territory. Suddenly, the "Bertrand" hit a snag or sandbar and split amidship. Although the boat sank in a matter of minutes, there was enough time for the crew and passengers to get off safely.

Some of the cargo was removed following its sinking, but any major salvage attempt was impossible due to the treacherous Missouri waters, and the shifting sandbars. Also, there were limited facilities available for this type of undertaking.

As the years rolled by, the river changed its course continually. Sand and silt covered the "Bertrand". The wreckage was left a mile away from the new channel. Records of its location were lost. The "Bertrand" was all but forgotten by most.

Stories still persisted, however, of gold and mercury in the boat's 4½ foot hold. It had been crammed with cargo at the time of the boat's departure from St. Louis. This included about $4,000 in gold and silver coins, about 450 steel flasks of mercury . . . worth about $250,000 today . . . 5,000 gallons of whiskey, and a variety of goods to be delivered to the Montana stores at Fort Benton.

In the fall of 1967, two men from Omaha . . . Jesse Purcell and Sam Corbino . . . obtained a permit from the government to search for the wreck of the "Bertrand". With the use of electronic metal-detecting equipment and core samples, they were able to locate the boat.

In February of 1968, test borings produced bits of wood, tin, lead, leather, and glass. They recovered the neck of a bottle which still had a strong odor of whiskey. The use of probes indicated a rough outline of a large boat. The "Bertrand" was 161 feet long.

In October of 1968, the site was excavated. A portion of the Hull of the "Bertrand" was finally exposed. Then came the task of removal of the cargo. One of the first items was a box of soap

from St. Louis labeled "Stores . . . Bertrand", which positively identified the boat that had sunk 103 years previously.

The hull was covered with about thirty feet of sand. Eighteen feet under the water table. It was

necessary to continually pump the excavation site to keep it dry while salvaging was in progress.

After the cargo was removed, the well points and pumps were pulled. It took only six hours for the excavated hole to refill.

An estimated two million items were removed from the cargo hold. It gave a good cross section of the 19th Century frontier life.

Under the salvage agreement with the government, nearly all the priceless cargo went to them. But only nine mercury flasks were recovered and the whiskey found was of no monetary value. No gold was discovered. The items the two salvagers kept went into a museum erected for that purpose.

CHAPTER ELEVEN

THE MORMON TREASURE TRAIL

here are many stories that the Mormons buried caches of valuables, relics, and artifacts along the trek west. A lot of them were on foot and when their belongings became too burdensome and heavy to carry any further, they stopped and buried them. The Mormons were in hopes that they might return someday and recover these caches.

There are stories that the elders, before leaving Nauvoo, Illinois, cached a lot of valuables under one of the buildings.

Nauvoo is a river town which sits atop a hill and presents a beautiful scene of a silver river and rolling hills in the warmer seasons of the year. It is about a mile across the mighty Mississippi from the town of Montrose, Iowa.

The Mormons started their westward trek during the wintertime . . . February of 1846, due to religious persecution. The temperature was zero and below. The river was frozen enough to allow many of them to cross by foot and wagon on the ice. Their first encampment, at the end of February, was at Sugar Creek, eight miles into the Iowa territory. Their spirits were low, but their leader, Brigham Young, was determined to move them beyond the mountains of the west. So, in March of 1846, 500 wagons left their camp at Sugar Creek. But part of the burdensome valuables were allegedly left near this encampment.

They decended to the Des Moines River Valley at Croton. Today, a graveled country road follows this trail. From there, they proceeded north through Farmington and the crossing at Bonaparte Mills.

The original Mormon Trail at Keosauqua is at the site of Indian Creek Camp, directly south of Lacey Keosauqua State Park's southern boundary. In the park, a marker shows a later group's crossing place. The original group left Keosauqua and proceeded west for eight miles to Richardson's Point, where they camped for a time. Here, also, they reportedly buried a ton of cannon ball and shot. They used trees as markers to the hiding place. The trees are now gone and the exact location of the cache, which has never been recovered, remains unknown.

There used to be a marker at Lebanon, which designated the trail, until someone stole it. But on a nearby farm, there is a gap in the undergrowth in a pasture, where the path enters the woods.

The trail leads to the Fox River Valley. The

Mormons usually followed rivers and streams, keeping close to water and woods, and camping on higher ground. About 1½ miles north of Bloomfield, in Davis County on Highway 63, on the west side of the road is a marker showing the site of an encampment. There are rumors of caches and relics buried in the vicinity.

At Drakesville is a road that the Mormons themselves had built in 1838, when they had been expelled from Missouri. Relics have been found in this area from both journeys.

Just before the end of March of 1846, the group had reached the Chariton River Valley, not too far from the northern boundary of Missouri.

Next, the journey led them to the town of Cincinnati, where they camped for two weeks in April. In 1947, a man from Missouri, camping in this area, found a small cache of coins. It is believed there is more.

Twelve miles to the west, the Mormons ran into difficulty. It is the western boundary of Appanoose County. Settlement was sparse, as the counties had not been charted and roads built. They sent some scouting parties ahead to determine the best route. They did not want to get 200 wagons into a place they would not be able to get out of.

The group went northwest, south of Harvard and then through Allerton. When the April rains turned the trail into a mire, they made only two or three miles a day. Their progress was slowed as the horses sunk to their bellies in the mud.

During this rainy period of time, they first made camp on Muddy Creek, just south of Humeston. They then pushed forward to a hill overlooking the Welden River Valley. Here, they established a settlement known as Garden Grove. The

group worked together cutting down trees, building cabins, splitting rails for fences and planting crops for those who were to follow . . . all in two weeks time!! Many relics and artifacts have been found scattered around this vicinity.

By now, the two months traveling in adverse conditions had weakened the group. Some were suffering from exposure and malnutrition. Others from whooping cough.

Although there is a cemetery-of-sorts in an open space below the memorial tablet at Garden Grove, there was not time or material for individual grave markers. Perhaps, as was the custom at the time, valuables were buried beneath the skeleton to ward off anyone trying to recover them.

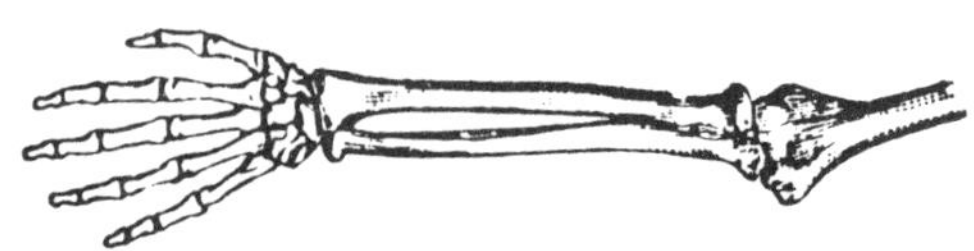

The trail progresses through the woods on the McTaggart property. There, deep ruts of the trace are visible.

From Garden Grove, the course angles northwest . . . between Welden and Van Wert. It then went into present-day Clarke County, through Murray and on into Union County.

In early June, the Mormons cleared 3,000 acres of land at a site north of Talmadge overlooking the Grand River. They planted crops and called the settlement Mount Pisgah. Although it is one of the best-known spots on the Mormon Trail in Iowa, it is also one of the hardest places to reach. County roads in this area are inadequately marked. The road that does provide the most direct access . . . the one north from Highway 34 . . . is in part dirt, and almost impassable in wet weather. Two men in the 1950's, while looking for mushrooms, discovered a sizable cache in this area.

There is another cemetery-of-sorts at Mount Pisgah. Sunken places in the mown ground mark the graves of hundreds of Mormons buried here. These graves cluster along the trail. There is a shaft monument in the cemetery.

From Mount Pisgah, the group continued westward. It was now June of 1846 and the going was easier. The trail leads north of Creston through Spaulding. Then to Orient in Adair County. The trail then heads in a westerly direction to the area south of Bridgewater. Here, the Mormon Lake State Park keeps their passage alive.

In Cass County, Edna Township, the cemetery is marked on the map, and a bronze plaque commemorates these Mormon pioneers.

South of Lewis is Cold Spring State Park. The park is thought to have been a 19th Century Indian pow-wow location. The ruts of the Mormon Trail is still visible on a hillside in the camping area. Both Indian and Mormon relics have been discovered here.

Mormons who came later, dug caves in the hillside of the Nishnabotna River Valley, which is a few miles to the west of Lewis. These caves were their winter homes. In the 1930's, some adventurous teenagers recovered a large number of relics from these caves.

After they crossed the Nishnabotna River, they traveled north as far as present-day Highway 6. Then turning southwest, they followed the course of streams to Macedonia.

At a county park west of town, the group had made camp and built a bridge across the west branch of the Nishnabotna River.

A four-day trip by wagon took the Mormons to the east bank of the Missouri River. They camped near the present-day Lake Manawa State Park south of Council Bluffs. There is no marker to designate this area, probably because a more important site lies across the river at Florence, Nebraska. It is known as the "Winter Quarters" and lies just north of Omaha.

In June of 1962, a small treasure was found north of Council Bluffs. Finders believe it was Mormon Treasure.

North on the interstate in Iowa is the Mormon Bridge which crosses the Missouri River.

At Florence, their encampment sat like a crown on top of a hill. The Mormons . . . remembering Nauvoo . . . felt it was more defensible. Also, they were in hostile Indian territory, without legal

right. But they stayed anyway, settling in for the winter by building cabins and digging caves in the hillside.

Although the Mormons fared better through that winter, death still took its toll of the population. Of the more than 3,000 who had arrived at Florence to spend the winter, over 600 died. Apparently, most of them were either very old or very young, as indicated on a bronze tablet at the base of the memorial.

A few years later, another group of Mormons was making their way to Salt Lake City by an easier route. They were aboard the sidewheeler "Saluda", traveling up the Missouri River. The boat met with heavy ice and a strong current on the north side of the river. They were forced to return to Lexington, Missouri, for the night.

The next day, the "Saluda" again tried to round

the point and was forced back. The captain then ordered all steam possible and tried for the third time. When the boat was about thirty feet from the shore, the boilers exploded! The boat had been loaded with passengers . . . about 250 of them Mormons. The passengers were blown to bits and scattered over the river and banks. Only a hundred were ever accounted for!!!

CHAPTER TWELVE

DEVIL'S NEST TREASURE CACHES

nox County, Nebraska, is in the northeastern corner of the state on the Missouri River. Seventeen miles north of Crofton (five miles north of Lindy, Nebraska or twenty-five miles southwest of Yankton, S.D.), is a tract of woodlands and rough meadow called Devil's Nest. In the Lewis and Clark Journals, it was referred to as Bonhomme Island.

This area is loaded with tales of outlaws, bandits, robbers and murderers who used it as a hideout and sanctuary from the law. It is claimed that there are hundreds of treasure caches here. Many of them have never been recovered.

The Devil's Nest area is dotted with caves used by the desperadoes for over seventy years. The Jesse James outlaw gang reportedly buried a large cache of gold and silver coins in this region.

Also, an 1800's outlaw by the name of Maguire buried a hoard of gold bars here.

In 1964, over $6,000 in gold and silver coins was found in several caches by a group from Omaha. Also, a man from Rapid City dug up a cache of brand new gold coins that he suspected was taken from a mint shipment.

Part of the site is now a state park and is submerged by waters of the Lewis and Clark Lake.

For metal detector enthusiasts, there are several unnamed ghost towns located in the rugged country around Devil's Nest.

CHAPTER THIRTEEN

THE MAGNIFICENT "ECLIPSE"

he steamboat "Eclipse" was a rather elegant boat. Built in 1852 at a cost of $120,000, she was the largest steamboat built in the west before the Civil War. The vessel was 350 feet long and weighed 1,117 tons. For several years the "Eclipse" was in a class all by herself. It was hailed as a wonder boat. Its accommodations were said to equal or surpass those in many of the best hotels of the country. It even had a full-sized bank vault which later caused this boat to be buried treasure.

The occasional decoration exuberance was illustrated in the saloon of the '"Eclipse". This was the dominating feature of the magnificent cabin and represented a blending of the Gothic and Norman

styles. The ceiling was divided into diamonds and half-diamonds by the crossing of the Gothic arches. At the points of intersection hung pendant acorns entwined with oak leaves of rich gilt. The whole gave the appearance of two vast, arched colonnades. The intervening spaces in the ceiling were decorated with frescoes.

Each stateroom door was embellished with a large landscape. Over the forward entrance to the cabin were two large paintings of her patron cities . . . Louisville and New Orleans.

The large stained-glass skylights above and the six massive and richly gilded chandeliers were objects of wonder as well as light.

She had a crew of 121 men, including 70 firemen and deckhands, 25 waiters and stewards, five cooks, three mates and five engineers, in addition to clerks, pilots, etc. . . with wages totaling over $4,600 a month.

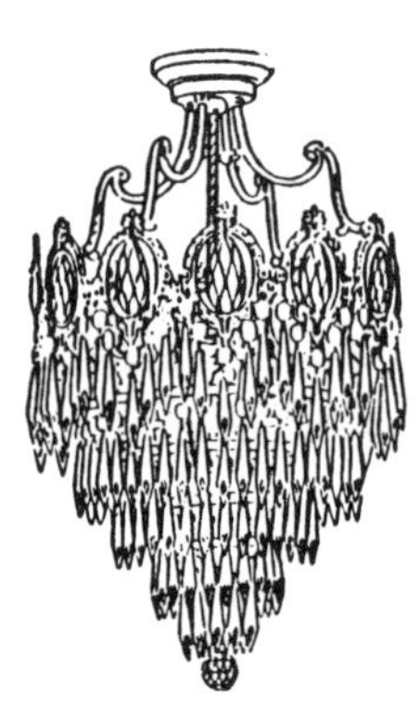

One of her claims to fame was a race with the "Shotwell" in 1853.

It is alleged that there was over a whiskey barrel full of newly-minted silver coins aboard the "Eclipse" when she met her fate on September 3, 1887, 15 miles below Sioux City, Iowa, sinking in the depths of the Big Muddy.

CHAPTER FOURTEEN

THE BURNT CREEK CACHE

ack in the early 1860's, a party of miners was returning by small boat from the Idaho and Montana gold fields. During the course of their journey down the Big Muddy one afternoon, they stopped at Fort Berthold. This was a post in the west central part of what is now North Dakota. That evening, while "shootin' the breeze," one of the miners freely confided to a trader stationed there that the party had a fortune in gold in their possession.

The men stayed a few days and then continued their trip downriver. Several days later, word came back to the fort that the party had been massacred by Indians somewhere along the east bank near Burnt Creek.

Records show that about 100 lodges of Dakotas,

which at that time were a very hostile group, were camped a short distance from the Missouri's banks. One of the Dakota hunters sighted the miners coming downriver. The hunter summoned the other warriors. The miners began to tie up to the river's edge to

make camp for the night. The warriors attacked and killed them, then scalped the men and rifled their bodies. Only one miner, a Frenchman, managed to escape. He later returned to the scene of ambush but was killed for his effort.

It is interesting to conjecture about the fortune in gold that the party had with them. It is claimed that after the trader the miner had boasted to, learned of the massacre he decided to make a trip to the scene of the ambush. He was accompained by a friendly Ree Indian. The trader just told the Indian that they were going to make an investigation but did not tell him of the gold.

Being very cautious, the pair located the place of slaughter. From the evidence, they concluded that the miners had stood up to step ashore from the boat. The gunfire had been so intense that it had sunk the aft portion of the craft. The bow was

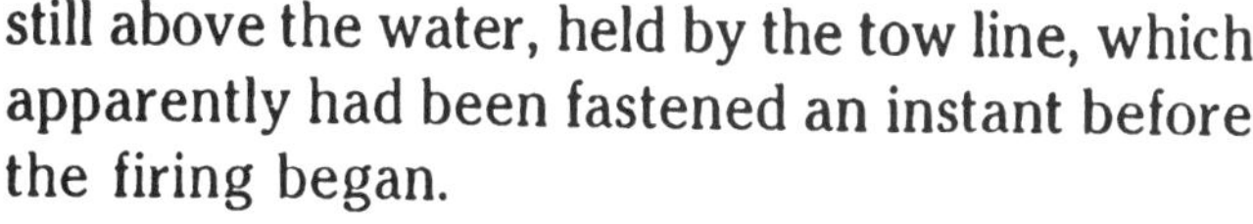

still above the water, held by the tow line, which apparently had been fastened an instant before the firing began.

On the excuse of needing fresh meat for supper, the trader sent his Indian companion into the woods. He then quickly searched the partially submerged boat. The man was rewarded by locating a hidden compartment which held the victims' gold. But knowing, because of its weight, that he would be unable to carry it all back to the post, he buried a great deal of it . . . what he could not carry on him . . . along the riverbank.

When the Indian returned, the trader told him that they might as well go back to Fort Berthold right away as there was nothing around the boat worth investigating. The Indian later admitted that the boat looked as if it had been hacked here and there, but he did not think anything of it at the time.

There is no record that the trader ever returned to recover the cache of gold, which has been estimated at over $75,000. If he did return, he apparently was never able to relocate the treasure, as he never displayed any large amount of gold at the fort.

Therefore, on the banks of the Missouri River, near the mouth of Burnt Creek, lies a cache that would be worth any treasure hunter's effort to locate!!

CHAPTER FIFTEEN

THE BOBBY GREENLEASE RANSOM MONEY

n Monday, September 28, 1953, six-year-old Bobby Greenlease was abducted from an exclusive Kansas City, Missouri, school. A red-haired woman, on the pretext that she was an aunt and that his mother was seriously ill, walked out with the first-grader.

They had caught a taxi-cab, and, according to the cab-driver, discussed Bobby's dogs and

parrot along the way. They then stepped out of the cab and vanished in a late model Ford bearing Kansas license plates.

After a night of helpless waiting, the distraught parents had still heard nothing from the stocky, red-haired woman.

Police Chief Bernard said, "We're treading lightly. We don't want the boy hurt."

He said that the police activity was being carried on strictly to the extent that the 71-year-old millionaire father, Robert C. Greenlease, and the 45-year-old socialite mother, Virginia Greenlease, would allow. The parents said they were ready to do anything to cooperate with the kidnappers to get Bobby back unharmed.

After two days of anxious waiting, and near collapse, the father offered the kidnappers a "blank

check" if they would return Bobby alive.

The FBI, who had by now entered the case, announced that $600,000 ransom had been paid by the frantic Mr. Greenlease less than a week after the kidnapping. They also advised that the body of little Bobby Greenlease, murdered by his abductors, was found in a shallow grave in St. Joseph, Missouri!!

Two persons were under arrest in St. Louis for the kidnap-murder. They were Mrs. Bonnie Brown Heady, a stocky, red-haired, 41-year-old alcoholic divorcee, and Carl Austin Hall, a 37-year-old former convict and black-sheep son of a prominent Kansas attorney. Hall was also an alcoholic and a drug addict. Both had criminal records.

Bonnie Brown Heady said she had been duped into participating in the crime but did say that she'd rather be dead than poor.

Carl Hall contended that he had picked up the ransom money but said the boy had been killed by Thomas John Marsh, who he said was a "tattooed desperado and child molester", but authorities did not believe Hall, as his story had too many inconsistencies.

Local and state police agencies did not issue an official arrest order for Marsh, although authorities in the Midwest and east conducted their own local searches for the "mystery man". Descriptions were published in newspapers and pictures shown on TV newcasts. Persons in Minnesota, Iowa, Illinois, Indiana, Michigan, and New York reportedly saw a man resembling Marsh.

A plump 22-year-old prostitute, Sandra O'Day, was held in the Jackson County jail at Kansas City as a material witness. Hall had accused her of stealing about $300,000 of the ransom money. She was not allowed to make her story public except on the witness stand.

Meanwhile, Missouri Governor Donnelly said an investigation was being made into the circumstances of Hall's parole from the Missouri State Penitentiary the previous April. He had served fifteen months of a five-year term for armed robbery.

Although the FBI in Washington said that it would not order a Federal search for Marsh until Hall's inconsistencies were "ironed out", they charged him with illegal flight to avoid prosecution.

Hall had stated that he left the boy with Marsh the day of the kidnapping and later found Bobby dead at Mrs. Heady's home in St. Joseph. Marsh had disappeared. Mrs. Heady gave an entirely different story.

Hall had also given conflicting stories of what happened to the missing half of the $600,000 ransom. He only had about $294,000 in his St. Louis hotel room at the time of his arrest. One story was that the prostitute had stolen it. Another version was that he had put it in a plastic bag and thrown it into a vacant lot. The authorities took Hall to this lot, where it was thoroughly searched, and only found an empty plastic bag.

Police believed that Hall had hidden the money somewhere in St. Louis after giving the prostitute he had spent the night with $1,000 and Mrs. Heady, $2,000.

A new investigation was ordered when it was revealed that the two suitcases of money found at the time of Hall's arrest did not arrive at the police station for more than an hour after the arrest. St. Louis Police Chief Jeremiah O'Connell

said he didn't think the missing half of the ransom had ever gotten to St. Louis after being picked up by the kidnap-slayers at a highway junction 10 miles east of Kansas City on the night of October 4.

The pair was returned to Kansas City to await formal grand jury indictment for violation of the Lindberg-kidnap law. After the indictment, they would then go on trial. A death sentence would result in their transfer to the state penitentiary at Jefferson City, as the federal government uses local facilities for its executions.

The police lieutenant who had arrested the kidnappers refused to testify before the federal grand jury, although he and his landlady had been summoned. He said he did not want to disclose the names of his informants. He then resigned from the police force because he couldn't stand the "castigation" of his character by rumors of handling of the case and his anger over a top-level police inquiry about the money.

A few days later, the ex-police officer and his landlady arrived in Honolulu, Hawaii. He stated that they were thinking about settling down there and as soon as he could get a divorce, they would marry.

On November 3, Carl Austin Hall and Bonnie Brown Heady pleaded guilty to the kidnap-murder of Bobby Greenlease. Their pleas moved them toward execution in the Missouri gas chamber.

Meanwhile, a hitchhiker killed in an automobile accident in Kentucky was identified as Thomas John Marsh, the man that Hall had at first accused of murdering Bobby but later cleared through his confession.

Hall had admitted shooting Bobby with a .38

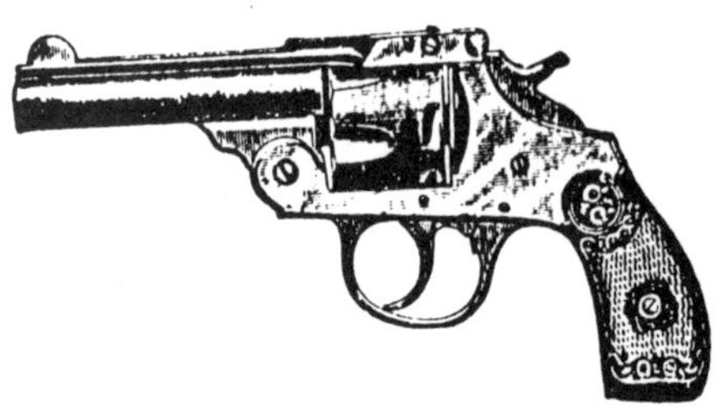

caliber gun just hours after Mrs. Heady had kidnapped him. They then buried him in Mrs. Heady's backyard and planted flowers over the

shallow grave. After that, they had collected the ransom money and left for St. Louis.

At one point during the trial, Hall had said he had bought two garbage cans and a shovel at a hardware store. He apparently had buried the money along the Meramec River bottoms in St. Louis. But he stubbornly insisted that he had been too drunk and doped up to remember the exact location. Officials centered their search in that area, but there is no record that any of this cache has ever been found!!!

On November 19, it took the federal jury only one hour and seven minutes to decide that the pair should be executed. They were sentenced to die in the gas chamber on December 18, 1953.

The great gray prison by the Missouri River at Jefferson City was quiet under a full moon the night of December 18. Warden Ralph Edison, at four and a half minutes past midnight, clanged home the two-foot steel lever that loosed a deadly almond-scented gas into the metal chamber. This painlessly and swiftly ended the lives of the desperate pair who had plotted and carried out one of the most heinious crimes of the 20th Century!!!

CHAPTER SIXTEEN

THE BANDY-LEGGED BUGGER

orth Dakota is a comparatively young state, having been admitted just over 100 years ago. Around that period of time, the white man and the Indian hunted the buffalo on the grass-covered prairies. Their fights for possession of this land were bloody and bitter.

When the railroads pushed their paths across the

prairie-land, they brought thousands of industrious homesteaders. These pioneers broke the sod, planted their grain and raised livestock. Life was not easy for these early settlers.

Although North Dakota is a prairie state, only the eastern part is flat. There are rolling and wooded hills in the central part and the western region is rugged hill country. Bismarck, the state capital, is located in the south-central part of this region on the Missouri River.

Around the turn of the century, the Old Rock Haven boat yard was located two or three miles north of Bismarck. Trappers and freighters congregated here when their boats were in need of repair.

One such trapper that appeared at Rock Haven one day was "Spunky" Sanders. His boat had hit a snag in "Big Muddy" and was taking on water. Luckily, he was able to keep it bailed out until he could make it ashore at the boat yard. There was considerable damage, but "Spunky" needed it to make a living. So, he left the boat for repairs and made his way to the local "watering hole" to slake his thirst.

"Spunky" was aptly named, as he had more guts than most men of much larger stature. He was about five-foot four, bony-thin, bandy-legged and grizzled. He had some front teeth missing, giving him a "jack-o-lantern" look when he grinned . . . which was often. "Spunky" chewed tobacco, which dribbled down into his gray-streaked beard, staining it a brownish-yellow. He didn't exactly have an aversion to water but seldom drank it or used it for personal cleanliness. Few people willingly stood downwind from "Spunky".

Although the saloon which he entered was crowded, the other customers gladly gave "Spunky" plenty of room. He honored them with his best toothless grin.

"Thanky kindly, podners," he said, moving in close to the bar. "Gimme a bottle of yer best "red-eye" and a glass. Ah done worked up a hell of a thirst!" he told the barkeep.

"Spunky" belted down about three-fingers of the whiskey, then licked his lips.

"Damnation! That shore is good stuff!" he told no one in particular, plunking down some gold coins in payment of the bottle. "Ah'll jest keep it. Shore duz make a body feel good all over!!"

"Spunky" downed the rest in his glass, then refilled it. Two of the men were eyeing him furtively but didn't want to get close enough to engage him in conversation.

They had seen his gold coins and were discussing him in low tones. The pair finally moved down the bar, closer to the odorous little trapper.

"Ya shore musta bin thirsty," Harry Hasco, one of the pair, casually observed.

"Ya speakin' ta me, podner?" "Spunky" inquired. "Iffen so, yah, ya jest might say thet. Had a hell of a trip downriver. Hitta snag and kinda tore up ma boat. Musta bailed 'bout haffa the river outen the thing."

"Are ya a prospector?" Jack Donnelly, the other half of the pair, asked.

"Nope. I'ma fur trapper," "Spunky" replied.

"Must do purty good, huh?"

"Oh, jest fair-ta-middlin', ah guess. What you fellers do?" he asked.

"Freighters," Harry replied. "Ship stuff up 'n down the Big Muddy. Had a li'l engine trouble."

"Spunky" belted down another slug of whiskey and wiped his mouth with the back of his hand. He was starting to feel the effects of the "red-eye" and was a little unsteady on his feet. Jack noticed this and suggested the trio find a table and sit down. The crowd had thinned out a bit, so they were able to find an empty table.

"You fellers stickin' around long?" "Spunky" inquired.

"Boat shud be ready fer us first thing in the mornin'," Jack replied. "Gotta git goin' then. Lost too damn much time a'ready. Gotta git all a thet stuff delivered."

"Don't know jist how long it'll take fer 'em ta fix mine. Too long, prob'ly," "Spunky" remarked.

"Well, what say we live 'er up tanite, then," Harry suggested.

"Sounds like purty good idear," the trapper remarked. "Gotta coupla things ah have ter do fust, though. Kin ah meetcha back here in 'bout a half-hour, okay?"

"Shore, why not?" Jack replied.

"Spunky' left the pair sitting in the saloon. He had not gotten a sleeping room in which to leave part of his gold coins. So, he walked into a wooded area a short distance from the saloon. There, he pulled out a disreputable looking handkerchief. Digging into his pockets, he put a handful of gold coins into the hanky, wrapping it around the money. He dug a shallow hole and concealed his cache with some of the loose dirt. Wiping his hands off on his pants legs, he returned to the saloon.

"Spunky" and his "friends" celebrated most of the night away. Some time before dawn, Harry suggested that it might be a good idea to get a sleeping room so they could take a nap before heading out on their trip. It was still quite dark when they left the saloon. There was no one else out and about. When they were out of earshot of anyone in the saloon, the pair of freighters grabbed "Spunky" by the arms. Harry put one hand over "Spunky's" mouth.

"Now, ya li'l bow-legged bugger, we wants yer money. And don't ya yell, nor give us a bit of trouble . . . or else!!"

"Spunky", taken totally by surprise . . . and being quite drunk . . . offered little resistance. Harry took his hand off the little man's mouth.

"Ah don't have very much on me," he slurred.

"Ah dunt b'lieve thet!" Harry countered. "Ya was spendin' them gold coins jest like they was goin' outta style!"

"Ah done spent mosta whet ah had," "Spunky" replied.

"Whatja do whin yer was gone?" Jack asked. "Hide 'em??"

When "Spunky" didn't answer, Jack hit him in the mouth with his fist.

"Damn yer hide!! Ya better tell us right here and now . . . didja hide 'em?"

"Yah, yah, ah done hid 'em. But ah cain't 'member jist whur!!"

"Dunt gimme thet!" Jack yelled, hitting "Spunky in the mouth again.

His already swollen mouth caused blood to run down into his beard. He was sagging at the knees, partly due to the whiskey. If the pair hadn't been holding his arms, "Spunky" would have fallen.

"Take it a li'l easy," Harry urged. "Iffen ya hit him agin, he won't be able ta tell us nothin'!"

"Ya gonna tell us whur ya hid them gold coins??" Jack yelled.

"Spunky" spluttered blood but did not say anything. Jack hit him hard in the stomach. "Spunky" retched and collapsed where he stood, blood spurting from his mouth. The pair stood looking down at him. "Spunky" wasn't moving!!

"Let's git the hell outen here!" Harry vehemently remarked. "I think ya done him in!!"

The pair of freighters hurried away, leaving the little bow-legged trapper lying near a large tree.

"Spunky's" body was discovered early that morning.

It was only luck that led the law to collar Harry later as part of a totally different crime.

Many other trappers and freighters had buried their valuables, too, so as not to be robbed. Wild celebrations were held, and like "Spunky", many never lived through them. So, there are many unrecovered caches in the region around the old boat yard.

One such cache was reportedly buried in 1926 by a bootlegger near the Rock Haven boat yard. There are no reports of the recovery of this $10,000 cache . . . all in $100 bills!!

CHAPTER SEVENTEEN

SUNKEN TREASURES OF THE MISSOURI

he Missouri River was not only very dangerous because of the snags, rapids, and sandbars, but because of its very powerful currents. Many boats ended up at the bottom of the river, and very few have ever been recovered.

Here are but a few of the approximately 400 boats lost in this river:

MISSOURI

Sometime prior to 1865, the "W.R. Caruthers" sank eight miles west of Mound City carrying $30,000 in gold coins in the ship's safe. In 1865, in about the same area, the "Sultanna" sank with $65,000 on board. Some sources claim that coins are occasionally washed ashore in this area.

In 1856, the steamboat "Sonora" sank at Portland with a cargo of furs, guns and gold bars worth $50,000. Nothing was ever recovered.

The sternwheeler, "Montana", was coming through the bridge at St. Charles on June 22, 1844, when it flanked into a pier and sank. A

portion of her cargo was salvaged. Some sources claim that the "Montana" carried a large quantity of gold and mercury on board and is one of the richest wrecks awaiting salvage on the Missouri River.

IOWA

In 1866, the steamboat "Mollie Dozier" struck a snag and sank a few miles below Council Bluffs. Over two hundred miners bringing back over $1,000,000 in gold dust and nuggets were aboard. Many miners were wearing gold-filled money belts. They were all drowned. The ship's safe was also filled with gold. There is no record of any recovery or salvage.

On July 18, 1897, the steamboat "Benton" was coming downstream toward the Sioux City drawbridge. The boat backed into some submerged piling. It partially sank and floated into the bridge, tearing off most of its upper cabin before sinking completely.

KANSAS

In 1856, the steamboat "Arabia" sank near Leavenworth. There have been gold coins found washed ashore on the Missouri River bank near the Leavenworth National Cemetery, thought to be from the wreck of the "Arabia".

In May of 1868, the steamboat "Aravian" snagged and sank, a total loss at Atchison.

NEBRASKA

In 1857, at the confluence of the Nemaha and Missouri Rivers, near Nemaha, a small boat carrying five returning California gold miners, overturned. It is claimed that the miners lost some $50,000 in bullion and gold coins in the accident.

In 1972, after a flood, a source claims that a large number of silver and gold coins were found along the west bank of the Missouri River, about ½ miles south of Nemaha.

SOUTH DAKOTA

It is claimed that coins have been found on the banks of the Missouri River just north of Chamberlain after severe flooding, probably washing ashore from a sunken steamboat.

On October 27, 1870, the "North Alabama" snagged above Vermillion in Bow River Bend. Her sinking caused the channel to change. Soon, the wreck was completely covered with sand and out of sight. In July of 1906, the channel again shifted, exposing the wreck.

On August 1, 1855, the "Kate Swinney", a 328-foot sidewheeler, snagged above the Vermillion River. It had a full cargo of furs on board. The crew was able to get ashore and started walking to Sioux City, Iowa. But, being saved from a watery grave, they were then attacked by Indians and killed.

NORTH DAKOTA

On July 17, 1892, the sternwheeler "Abner O'Neal" sank at Painted Woods and was listed as a total loss.

On June 16, 1896, the sternwheeler "Rose Bud" sank at the railroad warehouse at Bismarck. The river was falling rapidly at the time, causing the wreck to settle on submerged piling.

CHAPTER EIGHTEEN

LOST AND BURIED TREASURE

isted here are some more accounts of lost and buried treasures in the midwestern states. Some of them, where I could pinpoint the location, I have also included highways. Happy hunting!

MISSOURI

Rocheport is in the extreme southwestern corner of Boone County, on the Missouri River. It is the town claimed by the Confederate leader, Bill Anderson, as his capital. Loot from his raids is suspected as being cached in the area.

Old Franklin is across the river from Boonville and was the eastern terminus of the old Santa Fe Trail. Established in 1816, it was a ghost town by 1850 when outlaws, cattle rustlers and other criminals took it over, using it as a way station.

It is believed that several outlaw caches remain buried in this area that have yet to be recovered.

In recent years, there have been two spectacular Mexican gold coin caches found in this area by college students.

In 1927, a dying man confessed to having been a member of a gang that robbed a St. Louis jewelry store of $30,000 worth of jewels some

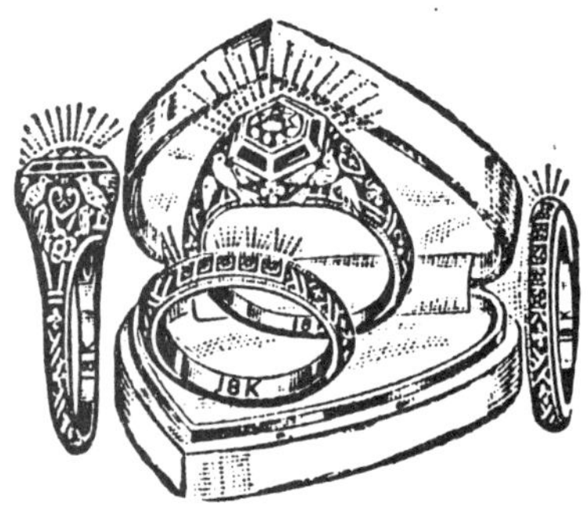

years earlier. He related that the haul had been buried between two large roots of an oak tree, and that his companions in the crime had been killed before they could recover it. He believed that the treasure had been buried in the suburb of Clayton, west of downtown St. Louis.

A large quantity of early 1800's U.S. and Spanish coins were found on the levee of the Missouri River near Hermann. A break in the levee had occurred during a flood in 1973. A dredge was used to repair the damage. Apparently, the coins were sucked up from the river bottom from the remains of a ship that had wrecked here. It is believed that a large cache may still remain here.

It is not known if the coins came from the wreck of the "Big Hatchie" who sank in 1843 after an explosion rocked her boiler room at Hermann. Many lives were lost in this accident. She went down, along with several hundred casks of mercury and kegs of whiskey. As far as records can confirm, there has been no salvage of this vessel.

Also, the sidewheeler ferry, "Washington", burned at Hermann on April 10, 1880.

Several treasure caches have been rumored to have been made by some very wealthy doctors in and around Savannah. At least one cache has been found.

In the 1920's, a bank robber is supposed to have buried $28,000 in currency in a fruit jar beside a tree, which was located about 100 feet north and east of a bridge southeast of Swope Park in Kansas City. While robbing another bank, he was captured and sentenced to twenty years in prison. After he was released, he returned to Kansas City, sure that he could recover the cache. But, not surprisingly, the park had expanded and the area was changed. He could never recover his cache. It is believed that the bridge in question is the one in today's Swope Park over the creek on Oldham Road.

Many prospectors and miners buried treasure caches on the outskirts of St. Joseph, which was the terminus of the Pony Express Route, as well as the departure point for the Oregon Trail and goldfields of California. The area was a frequent point of attack and robbery and much treasure is believed to remain cached in the region.

IOWA

Numerous treasure caches are reportedly buried in Stone Park and the hills overlooking the bend in the Missouri River at Sioux City. In 1957, a park worker found a cache of silver dollars. In 1959, a large cache of money and raw gold was found in the park. This area has been a treasure hunter's paradise in recent years.

Jesse James is known to have spent the winter of 1872-1873 in the rural village of Weston, where he wintered his horses. This is in Pottawattamie County. Some researchers believe that some of his outlaw loot remains cached in this area.

There is a story which claims that $35,000 in gold coins was buried near Weston by an outlaw in the 1800's, but it is not known if this cache is one of Jesse James' or not.

KANSAS

In 1891, G.G. Fox, while digging a site for a new ice house on his farm near Highland in Doniphan County, unearthed an eight-inch square iron box filled with foreign gold and silver coins. Local citizens believed he found a small portion of a much larger treasure cache that still remains buried on the property.

In a robbery of the post office at Alexandria in 1856, $1,000 in gold coins were stolen. Soldiers from nearby Fort Leavenworth gave chase and forced the outlaws to bury the loot somewhere along a deep slough on Stranger Creek in a heavy stand of timber. A few of the bandits were captured and the others escaped, but none ever returned to recover the cache.

In the 1920's, a treasure was recovered from a cornfield on a farm a couple of miles north of Springdale. Residents in the area claim that there were "mysterious lights" which had appeared previous to finding the treasure, but that they disappeared after the cache was recovered.

Some people believe that these mystery lights sometimes indicate a cache is buried in the vicinity.

NEBRASKA

It is rumored that a group of unidentified travelers buried a cache of treasure at the base of a lone tree somewhere along the Missouri River near Ponca, in Dixon County, in the northeastern corner of the state.

After the attempted bank robbery at Northfield, Minnesota, some of Jesse James' gang used Robbers Cave, which is located on the bluff along the Missouri River near Macy. They used it as a hideout for a while. It is believed that a cache of buried treasure was left in or near the cave. This site is in Thurston County, southeast of Winnebago in the northeastern part of the state; southwest of Sloan, Iowa, and due north of Decatur, Nebraska.

During the 1860's and 1870's, the Missouri River

ferry at Decatur was one of the most profitable businesses in the entire state. The tollkeeper kept his receipts in nail kegs, and when they were full, he buried them alternately in the surrounding Nebraska and Iowa hills near the ferry site.

A partially-filled nail keg was found in 1926 by a county supervisor and a grader-operator about 4 miles south of Decatur on the old river bottom road. The others have not been recovered.

Treasure hunters found a tobacco can half-full of large-sized gold-backed currency at Decatur. A baking powder tin full of gold coins was what the treasure hunters were searching for but failed to find it at the same location.

The owner of an 1860's hat factory at DeSoto (a ghost town four miles southeast of Blair, on the Missouri River along the old Omaha/Decatur Road) accumulated a fortune from his

business during the Civil War. He distrusted banks and buried his hoard of gold coins. He died before revealing the location of his gold and it was never recovered.

A family traveling in a wagon train buried their money sometime back in the middle 1800's. As was the custom of the time, it was buried for safekeeping at a campsite near Nebraska City, in Otoe County. The following morning they were unable to find the exact spot and had to abandon the cache as the wagon train continued the westward journey.

It is alleged that the Jesse James outlaw gang buried a cache of stolen treasure three miles southeast of Nebraska City at a site located on the present-day Catron-Miyoshi Fruit Farm. Two small treasurer caches have been recovered by treasure hunters at this location. It is believed that there is more.

Just after crossing the Missouri River near Rulo (Richardson County), a party of early pioneers was attacked by Indians. The only survivor was a small girl who stated many years later that the wagon train treasure of gold coins had been buried at the foot of a tree just before the massacre. The cache has yet to be found.

A restaurant owner in Fremont hid money all over Dodge County. His largest cache recovered so far was found in a flower bed in the backyard of his residence in the city. Much more is suspected.

In 1855, a hard-working blacksmith named Al Medley came to a small settlement in southeastern Nebraska by the name of Peru. Before too many months had passed, the blacksmith was able to put a few gold coins in a bank. This bank was in the ground. It is believed to be a cache of $1,000 to $2,000 at the time but would be worth much more today.

A good place to start looking is in the area around the old blacksmith shop and store. Also, you could check the Missouri River bank near where he operated his ferry. Wherever the cache is, it has eluded searchers for over a century and is well worth the hunting.

Horsethief Henry "Deadwood Hank" Ryan operated in and around the present-day Douglas County area. He once claimed that he had robbed an express car of gold coins outside of Omaha. According to "Deadwood Hank", most of the treasure was cached in the Fontanelle Forest. Some researchers have discounted this treasure as being non-existent but there are a good many treasure seekers who still search for this hoard.

SOUTH DAKOTA

In Brule County, the Nelson Roadhouse was a trading post at Nelson (which is now a ghost town midway between Pukwana and Chamberlain). It was a busy settlement during the gold rush days in the 1870's. It is now known as Custer's Farm. It has been reported that several caches of treasure were made here, some of which may still be buried.

In 1960, a historian investigated General Custer's activities here and stumbled onto some treasure leads. He found one cache and others have been found here since.

Several worthwhile treasure are thought to be hidden in and around the ghost town of Bloomington, in Clay County, about 4 miles north of Vermillion. Bloomington was once a thriving community but was destroyed by a band of outlaws in 1877.

NORTH DAKOTA

A Mandan Indian village was located one mile north of Menoken, also the location of a fort built by early French explorers. Many relics and artifacts can be found in the area. Menoken is a ghost town 10 miles east of Bismarck in Burleigh County. It is still shown on some maps. The Menoken Historic Site is just north of Hwy. 94.

Several valuable caches have been found in the area of old Fort Clark on the south bank of the Missouri River near the present town of Fort

Clark. It is believed that there is an especially valuable gold cache where miners returning from the Montana gold fields hid it. The American Fur Trading Co. founded a trading post here in 1829.

There are several forts and Indian villages in the area of Morton and Burleigh Counties, where many relics, artifacts, and caches have been found:

A Mandan Indian village was located on the bluffs along the Missouri River, northeast of Mandan.

An Indian village was located on the Heart River two miles southwest of Mandan.

Fort McKeen, a/k/a Fort Abraham Lincoln, was located six miles south of Mandan at Fort Lincoln State Park on State Highway 6, on the west side of the Missouri River.

Fort Rice is located on the Missouri River just south of the town of Fort Rice, on Highway 1806 on the west side of the river. It was built in 1864 by General Sully to protect the settlers.

In 1877, outlaws robbed a trader's pack train of a large cache of gold coins on the east side of the Missouri River near Raub. (Raub is now a ghost town, located sixteen miles south-southeast of Parshall, near Lake Sakakawea. Although it is considered a ghost town, it is still shown on some maps and is located on State Highway 37.) The packers took off after the bandits and killed them after a few miles chase, but the gold coins were not found. It is believed that the coins were buried or hidden somewhere along the short escape route. The treasure is still there!!

CHAPTER NINETEEN

INDICATORS

here exists a unique method to go treasure hunting without the use of a metal detector!! It is called "geobotanical prospecting" and uses trees, plants, and grasses (growing in their natural state) as indicators for locating water and mineral deposits. Here are a few:

Regardless of where you might find swamp grass, willow trees, or cattails, they indicate water. The Egyptians used this method of dowsing for water.

Holly trees and hemlock sometimes indicate there is a deposit of lead beneath their roots.

Peppergrass and milk vetch often indicate the present of uranium in the area.

The wild poppy flower almost always indicates a copper deposit.

Although the horsetail plant's chief value is as an indicator of gold in a certain location, it does have the ability to extract gold from the ground if present.

It is believed that the early Spanish Jesuit priests practiced geobotanical prospecting in our Southwest. That is probably one reason why they were so successful in finding silver and gold deposits.

Although the art of prospecting by this method has been used for many, many years, there has been little written on the subject.

CHAPTER TWENTY

RESEARCH

esearch is one of the most important parts of any successful venture, be it treasure hunting or writing a book. Although it may sound discouraging, endless hours must be spent in obtaining information. But this is a wise investment of time before you invest money on expensive treasure hunting equipment or do any looking for those caches.

Libraries are probably your best source and the librarian, your best friend. Tell her what you are looking for . . . not necessarily that you are trying to find a treasure cache . . . but the area that you are researching. She might know exactly the book, brochure, state or county publication, etc., that would contain the needed information.

Card indexes can provide titles of books under listed subjects, or authors. If the library does not have the book you need, if you have the title and author's name, they can usually get it for you through the interlibrary system on loan.

Each book you review should have a list of references where the author obtained certain information. This could also give you further books to review.

If you have the correct date of an occurrence, most libraries have copies of old newspapers on microfilm. But be realistic in expecting to find a record of an event which happened too long ago.

Most libraries have a room devoted to state and local history . . . sometimes called the genealogy room. You can find books of existing histories, state and county maps, journals and census records. If you need topological maps which the library does not have, they can be obtained through the government at little or no cost.

Also, most libraries have a State Department of Transportation book of maps listed by county.

They can either be photocopied (though they are usually large enough to require several copies and then pieced together) or ordered through the state. These are convenient to have if highlighted with a yellow marker on areas you want to research, such as “ghost towns”.

If you are researching a house in town that is no longer in existence, an old city map may be a valuable aid to locate the site. Also, old city directories and plat maps are helpful.

Museums and historical societies can sometimes provide you with information of value that could not be found elsewhere.

Senior citizens can be a very good source of information and can usually remember events that younger persons never heard of. Especially, the local historians remember how a town or area has changed, and the way it used to be. And they are more inclined to talk with you than others might be.

Make photocopies of things that you may need. It is much easier to refer back to and saves a return trip to the library.

The library usually has a book on abandoned or "ghost towns" in the area or perhaps for the entire state. I have found, through my research, the names and locations of over 8,000 such towns in the Midwest.

If you are researching old fort sites, there is usually a book which covers a certain region, such as forts along the upper Missouri River, etc.

There are countless other ways to do research. Subscribe to certain magazines that covers the subject you are researching.

Historical markers along highways provide a good source of information. Old family histories, court records, old letters or diaries can also provide limitless information.

If you are a metal detector enthusiast, winter can be an excellent time to do your research. Check out your locations, get your maps together, contact people. Then prepare your equipment, seeing that it is in good working order. Plan your trip carefully.

ONE GOOD RESEARCH TIP: History doesn't always agree on the manner in which events occurred . . . nor do the alleged experts that record these events!! But no matter how exaggerated they seem, almost all stories, legends, etc. are based on fact. Try to get as much available information on a treasure site as possible from different sources, as there is always room for error!

As one professional treasure hunter said, there is nothing that can stir the human heart and imagination so much as the lure and fascination of hidden riches!!

EPILOGUE

So, yet today, the waters and the banks of the Missouri River hide secrets from us. Among the secrets are caches of gold and silver. Jars of mercury and barrels of whiskey lie buried, ready for the adventurous with information or good fortune a little better than others'.

Relics from another time await the turn of the shovel or the glint of the sunlight to rejoin us today.

INDEX

If you have enjoyed this book, perhaps you would enjoy others from Quixote Press.

HUMOR:

Iowa's Roadkill Cookbook	B. Carlson	7.95
South Dakota's Roadkill Cookbook	B. Carlson	7.95
Missouri's Roadkill Cookbook	B. Carlson	7.95
Minnesota's Roadkill Cookbook	B. Carlson	7.95
Wisconsin's Roadkill Cookbook	B. Carlson	7.95
Illinois' Roadkill Cookbook	B. Carlson	7.95
How to Talk Midwestern	R. Thomas	7.95
A Field Guide to Missouri's Critters	B. Carlson	7.95
A Field Guide to Iowa's Critters	B. Carlson	7.95
A Field Guide to Illinois' Critters	B. Carlson	7.95

MISCELLANEOUS:

Memoirs of a Dakota Hunter	G. Scholl	9.95
Hitchhiking the Upper Midwest	B. Carlson	7.95
Me 'n Wesley (about homemade toys on the farm)	B. Carlson	9.95
Iowa, The Land Between the Vowels (farmboy tales)	B. Carlson	9.95
Iowa's Early Home Remedies	various	9.95
Illinois' Early Home Remedies	various	9.95
Missouri's Early Home Remedies	various	9.95
Underground Iowa (tales from under Iowa's soil)	B. Carlson	9.95
Underground Illinois	B. Carlson	9.95
Underground Missouri	B. Carlson	9.95
Early Iowa Schools	C. Johnston	9.95
Tricks We Played in Iow	Various	9.95

OUTHOUSES:

Iowa's Vanishing Outhouse	B. Carlson	9.95
Missouri's Vanishing Outhouse	B. Carlson	9.95
The Dakota's Vanishing Outhouse	B. Carlson	9.95
Wisconsin's Vanishing Outhouse	B. Carlson	9.95
Minnesota's Vanishing Outhouse	B. Carlson	9.95
Illinois' Vanishing Outhouse	B. Carlson	9.95

ROMANCE:

Old Iowa Houses, Young Loves	B. Carlson	9.95

MIDWEST RIVERBOAT SERIES:

Jack King vs. Detective MacKenzie	N. Bell	9.95
River Sharks & Shenanigans	N. Bell	9.95
Lost & Buried Treasure of the Mississippi	Scholl/Bell	9.95
Lost & Buried Treasure of the Missouri River	Bell	9.95
Romance on Board	H. Colby	9.95

MISSISSIPPI RIVER:

Mississippi River Po' Folk	P. Wallace	9.95
Strange Folks Along the Mississippi	P. Wallace	9.95
Mississippi River Cookin' Book	B. Carlson	11.95

GHOST STORIES:

Ghosts of the Miss. River, from Mpls. to Dub.	B. Carlson	9.95
Ghosts of the Miss. River, from Dub. to Keokuk	B. Carlson	9.95
Ghosts of the Miss. River, from Keokuk to S.L.	B. Carlson	9.95
Ghosts of Des Moines County, Iowa	B. Carlson	12.00
Ghosts of Scott County, Iowa	B. Carlson	12.95
Ghosts of The Amana Colonies, Iowa	L. Erickson	9.95
Ghosts of Polk County, Iowa	T. Welch	9.95
Ghosts of the Iowa Great Lakes	B. Carlson	9.95
Ghosts of Northeast Iowa	R. Hein et al.	9.95
Ghosts of the Black Hills	T. Welch	9.95
Ghosts of Door County, Wisconsin	G. Rider	9.95
Ghostly Tales of Southwest Minnesota	R. Hein	9.95
Ghosts of Rock Island County, Illinois	B. Carlson	12.95

LADIES OF THE EVENING:

Some Awfully Tame, But Kinda Funny Stories About:

—Early Iowa Ladies-of-the-Evening	B. Carlson	9.95
—Early Illinois Ladies-of-the-Evening	B. Carlson	9.95
—Early Wisconsin Ladies-of-the-Evening	B. Carlson	9.95
—Early Minnesota Ladies-of-the-Evening	B. Carlson	9.95
—Early Missouri Ladies-of-the-Evening	B. Carlson	9.95
—Early Dakota Ladies-of-the-Evening	B. Carlson	9.95

Need A Gift?

For

• Shower • Birthday • Mother's Day •
• Anniversary • Christmas •

Turn Page for Order Form

(Order Now While Supply Lasts!)

To Order Copies Of

Lost & Buried Treasures of the Missouri River

Please send me ______ copies of **Lost & Buried Treasures of the Missouri River** at $9.95 each. (Make checks payable to **QUIXOTE PRESS.**)

Name ________________________________

Street ________________________________

City ________________ State ______ Zip ______

Send Orders To:
QUIXOTE PRESS
31798 K18S
Sioux City, IA 51109

- -

To Order Copies Of

Lost & Buried Treasures of the Missouri River

Please send me ______ copies of **Lost & Buried Treasures of the Missouri River** at $9.95 each. (Make checks payable to **QUIXOTE PRESS.**)

Name ________________________________

Street ________________________________

City ________________ State ______ Zip ______

Send Orders To:
QUIXOTE PRESS
31798 K18S
Sioux City, IA 51109